MW01610710

THE LAST NEANDERTHAL

PITT POETRY SERIES

Ed Ochester, Editor

THE LAST
NEANDERTHAL

MICHAEL VAN WALLEGHEN

University of Pittsburgh Press

The publication of this book is supported by a grant from the Pennsylvania Council on the Arts.

Published by the University of Pittsburgh Press, Pittsburgh, Pa. 15261
Copyright © 1999, Michael Van Walleghen
All rights reserved
Manufactured in the United States of America
Printed on acid-free paper
10 9 8 7 6 5 4 3 2 1

Library of Congress Cataloging-in-Publication Data and acknowledgments are located at the end of this book.

A CIP catalog record for this book is available from the British Library.

For Pamela and Emily Lynn

CONTENTS

1

CLARITY

We rented our vacation cottage
every summer of my childhood
from the same glum farmer—

a giant, cadaverous Chippewa
with ten children, who never
seemed to look at us at all.

We paid the rent, picked up
the oars for our rowboat
then drove uncertainly off

through his dolorous chickens
to whatever slapdash hovel
matched the number on our oars.

No running water, no electricity
and no gas either that I remember.
A wood stove maybe, an outhouse

but inevitably a place so small
and flimsy, so chipped or bent
in each detail, it seemed to us

just charming, doll–like really—
as if it might have been a diorama
in some museum of natural history.

Except that starting now of course
we'd have to live there. Hornets
bats, the snake in the cupboard . . .

Take it easy, mother said. *Relax.*
She was born and raised up here
when northern Michigan was still

a dream–time, howling wilderness
of cold starvation and diphtheria.
She'd chop that snake to pieces.

And then she'd tuck me into a bed
exactly like the one she slept in
as a child. Every night, the same

huge shadows on the walls, the same
crickets, owls, and scrambling mice . . .
until once I even dreamt till dawn

that I could hear her baby sister
coughing. They gave her turpentine
I think, with lots of sugar in it

but she died anyway. That's why
at first light, there was so much
fog on the black water. No one

was up yet. Under our green boat
pulled halfway up on the beach
where the giant boatman left it

I found a brilliant leopard frog
beside a tiny, coal–black bullhead.
How still, how exquisite they look

even now, after all these years . . .
having achieved, in the mind's eye
the perfect clarity of last things.

TWO SEIZURES

I. THE SHOTGUN IN THE WEEDS, 1952

We're on vacation again—
two weeks at our favorite cottage
on murmurous Whitefish Lake . . .

where I'm lying face down
drying off after a swim
on the dimly booming raft
of planks and oil drums
we share with the neighbors.

My father is off somewhere
fishing in the green boat . . .

but mother is close by.
I can hear her playing
with my little brother
on the screened–in porch.

Meanwhile, it's important
that I keep one eye glued
to a hole in the planking . . .
because something down there
is scaring the sunfish—

a nervousness, an agitation
they betray in the fine tremor
of their ghostly, translucent
fins and tails . . .
                      a certain
wary, sidelong distance maybe
they keep from something
barely moving in the weeds—

those rags of cold, slimy grit
I hate to touch when diving
even with my toes.

And so the day proceeds—
a kind of underwater movie
deliberately unfolding scene
by scene, as I remember it

with an almost epileptic
slow–motion clarity:

first, my mother screaming
then blindness, water glare
the irrelevant, high kestrel
stalled against the light . . .

until I see
         my brother there
motionless and face down
beside his plastic inner tube
twenty feet from shore—

a seizure he narrowly survives
until we find him dead for sure—
forty years later, a suicide
in a rented basement.
                Nevertheless
in my dreams at least
he often dies by drowning—

down there in the weedy dark
where father, unaccountably
keeps his brand–new shotgun

and the yellow anchor rope
just simply disappears.

2. BEDTIME, 1992

In another of those hysterical
bedtime movies I'm sometimes
forced to watch, teetering

on the tricky brink of sleep
my brother turns up drunk again

humiliated by his stupid life
and collapses snoring in a chair
that will probably catch on fire

at any moment, like his couch
like half the furniture he owns

unless I can remove his cigarette
gently now, without waking him up
and perhaps triggering a seizure

which brings us both into Emergency
of course, where suddenly I'm yelling

at a sobbing nurse about insurance—
the same nurse my tied–down brother
has just convulsively bitten. Meanwhile

he could die at any moment and needs
to be admitted, insurance or not . . .

at which point, if it's not raining
or thirty below zero, it's probably
a good idea to get up and walk the dog

look up at the stars, remember him
in grade school, doing his homework

at the kitchen table. He's good
at math. If he could just concentrate
he'd get A's in everything. But already

he's staring blankly off at something
shining there beyond his own reflection

in the black and frozen window. His lips
are blue. And everything he's written
in his spiral notebook is backwards,

upside down, like writing in a mirror—
a language only the inscrutable window

or the stars themselves can read.
Then it's my job to put him to bed.
But first I have to remove his pencil

and give him a spoonful of medicine—
medicine he's too tired to swallow

sitting there on his top bunk bed
the TV blaring from the living room
and the same stars then as later—

when they carry out the body bag—
shining through the frozen trees.

PERPETUAL MOTION

When I was about ten
my friend Orville and I
stumbled on the secret
of perpetual motion.

It was all hydraulics—
hydraulics and gravity:

a series of bottles buried
at slightly different levels
in a hill of cement–mixing sand
behind our gargoyled church
and connected by tubes.

Water dribbled from level
to level and back again
without ever stopping—

a miracle of engineering
right up there with Holland
we thought, the human heart

or those alien–built canals
we'd read about on Mars.

Every day after school
that whole feverish autumn
of close rising, varicose moons
and leukemia's first symptoms—

shuddering chills, tiredness
his sweaty hair and pallor—

we dug it up, adjusted it
and watched the red-dyed water
pouring back and forth, back

and forth for hours . . .
                              till dark
imperceptibly falling, falling
once more surprised us there
rapt as Druids at prayer
on our little grave–sized hill—

high priests of the goddess moon
on whom the tides depend, guardians
of the sluice and watergate,
wizards of perpetual motion . . .

as if, at any minute now,
behind Assumption Grotto Church
and more imaginable than death,
starlit Stonehenge might appear—

next to the hole in the ground
they'd dug for a new addition
to our grade-school convent.

THE ELEPHANT IN WINTER

During the winter of course
they kept the elephant inside.

His "house," or dungeon really
was practically hidden by brush

and backed up to a small canal
just off the intricate main canal

behind Detroit's Belle Isle Zoo
on which you could skate for miles—

forever, if you happened to forget
in a rattling wind beyond surmise

or earshot of the lost pavilion
just which way you'd come exactly

now that all the trees were dark—
the footbridge wrong completely . . .

And it's right about here, in little
thudding intervals at first, I felt

the ice begin to move. Okay, sure
I thought: Snow trucks. The muffled

banging of some inscrutable pump
or boiler maybe . . . until, apropos

of nothing but that, a full–grown
male elephant goes suddenly berserk

a scant ten feet away, the whole
five–ton, concussive bulk of him

exploding into high–pitched screams
and a scattering of creeper twigs

every time he throws himself, *ka–boom!*
against the icy wall he lived behind.

That much at least is crystal clear.
But afterwards . . . I don't know. Perhaps

I fainted or went into shock somehow—
only to be rescued later by wolves . . .

Or maybe my father showed up finally
blinking his tiny, puzzled headlights

right where he was supposed to meet me
a good two hours ago with the car . . .

But isn't that the way with children?
Things that must have truly happened

end up blurred, inextricably confused
with dreams—so that, years later

a prized inheritance, a china cabinet
tinkling with the dishes and crystal

my mother only used at Christmas
eerily recalls, as much as anything

that dreamlike moment on the ice . . .
or the labyrinth, in fact, of home itself—

the angry stirring of the Minotaur
whom I've just woke up somehow

and now, by Christ, he's had enough—
whose least footstep shakes the house.

STARTLED AWAKE ONCE MORE
IN THE CITY OF DREAMS

> I can hear the bed groan and his shoes drop
> one by one. You can have it, he says.
> —Philip Levine, "You Can Have It"

In this dream I know is just a dream
I'm fifteen and every day after school
I go to work at Hudson's, a department store

in downtown Detroit. I'm a stockboy there.
I unload trucks, wrestle racks of dresses
men's suits and expensive children's wear

to their various, far–flung destinations
or hide out with my buddies smoking Camels
and tossing back tiny bottles of Chivas Regal—

miniatures for some executive blowout probably
that never make it off the freight elevator . . .
Great scotch! I wheeze inaudibly. *Smooth*

a strangled little voice pipes back. Then
we throw the empties down the package chute.
Finally, with eerie, cuckoo–clock precision

one kid vomits down the package chute: time
to punch out and catch the streetcar home . . .
It's always snowing in this dream—just cold

enough to change brief slush to iron rubble.
But it's oddly Christmas too, the streets
festooned with wreaths and blinking lights—

so that the goddamn streetcar, when it comes
is packed with tired shoppers, every seat
every strap and greasy stanchion occupied

by twins it seems—people at once themselves
and this entirely separate, dreamlike other
I too felt partnered by. Meanwhile, suddenly

I can't stand up. I have to kneel down now
and lay my head in some old lady's lap . . .
I can feel her cool hand against my cheek.

When she leans down and sings to me in Polish
I think I understand it . . . But of course
I'm only dreaming of this tender lullaby

this song that promises when I wake up again
two miles past my stop, it won't be me
who has to walk home with a hole in his shoe—

it won't be me listening to the plastic flags
of a dozen used car lots popping in the wind . . .
but someone cold sober, who doesn't dream at all.

CUCKOO

Katherine was born in Finland
and all her dithery life, childless

next door to us on Loretto Street
in rose–puttering, backyard Detroit

she'd suddenly remember things
out loud and apropos of nothing

from some dim, lost forest there—
the eyes of reindeer for example

blizzards, the aurora borealis
or puckering up as for a kiss

the crying of the cuckoo birds . . .
But then she'd be embarrassed

and change the subject, admiring
in these startled, blinking moments

my mother's iris maybe, or noting
how, in my delinquent adolescence

and sneering pompadour, I looked
so wondrously more like Elvis

every day. Her late husband Fred
was a fireman: fat, red suspenders . . .

a Rockwell illustration almost.
And once, when I was about ten

looking around, watching closely
he showed me a picture he'd taken

of a black man hanging from a tree
down South somewhere—assuming

in his twinkling, Kris Kringle way
that I shared his taste precisely . . .

I never said another word about it.
Not even to my mother. But Katherine

and I grew oddly chummy after that.
Katherine with her thick accent

her soggy pies and coffee cakes
her desperate need for company . . .

I remember the last time I saw her
I was home on leave from the navy.

I'd brought her a ceramic teapot
from Japan. She was in her driveway

shuffling back and forth, back
and forth, talking to the ants

shouting at the airplanes. She
had no idea who I was. Finally

another woman, her sister I think
came out and took her back inside.

That would have been back in 1957
but I remember it like yesterday . . .

That year, there were reindeer
in all the mountain meadows

and everywhere you could hear
the crying of the cuckoo birds—

two notes, then two notes returning . . .
the locally famous signal of lovers

who have to sneak out of the house
at nightfall and meet in the forest

where there are wolves and bears . . .
also the beast–men with their hoods

and torches, their terrible shadows
flickering like fathers and brothers.

GUARDIAN ANGEL

Mine had the look of someone
who slept in restaurant Dumpsters
or in the lube pit of some garage.

His hair a rat's nest, shirt
and Levi's stiff with grease

his work-smashed nails packed
with dirt, his idiot face
a drear, industrial gray . . .

But for the most part he kept
himself invisible, preferring

to look like nothing at all—
a clump of winter darkness maybe
stirring behind me in homeroom

or that curious, watery shadow
I'd catch odd moments wobbling

between my lathe and the wall
in machine shop—impatient, bored
waiting for my own long hair

to catch in the face plate
or for my own face in fact

to vanish in a spray of blood—
one of those dimwit accidents
our teacher kept shouting about

a thing he'd seen just happen
to any number of jerks like us.

And wincing through those lectures
those litanies of shredded meat
I'd hear, sometimes, that peculiar

drawn–out sigh that meant perhaps
to everyone but me, an ordinary bus

or streetcar merely, disappearing
back into the void of sad Hamtramck.
But it was him, of course . . .

a yawn he'd practiced for eternity.
And one sixth hour, in metal fitting

where an oxygen tank exploded once
I thought I heard him speak out loud:
Let's get this over with, he said

but whispering now, like acetylene
hissing from my welding torch . . .

He knew it was simply a question
of time, that my fate was sealed
that soon enough I'd look like him

or worse, like my uncle Freddy
my hands all amputated nubs . . .

So why not blow the place up?
It was something to think about
as injuries popped and sparked

with white–hot, angelic logic
against my pulled–down visor.

BEAUTY

for W. D. Snodgrass

> There is nothing so beautiful as that which
> does not exist.
> —Paul Valéry, *The Art of Poetry*

After I got out of the navy
I loafed at home for awhile
then enrolled myself in college . . .

I wanted to make something of myself—
become an accountant like my cousin

or, sweet Jesus, a lawyer. But somehow
(who knows what happens to our dreams?)
I found myself writing poems instead.

I was taking a class in poetry writing
and wrote whenever I could—all night

after my job loading trucks sometimes
at a card table down in the basement . . .
But when the sun came up, how odd

how astonishing it was, to realize
that time had simply disappeared!

And there, in front of me, timeless
for all I knew, the night-born poem:
"Seabent," I remember one beginning

"with slowly beating wings
the sunwashed seabirds pass . . ."

Reading it out loud made me dizzy
and I carried it around in my pocket
for days—although, at the same time

what I really felt soared impatiently
beyond words somehow. "Sunwashed

seabirds?" What kind were they exactly?
And where in that truck-loading life
had I stood enthralled to watch them?

Some snot-beaked, garbage-eating gulls
down by the Detroit river maybe . . .

Or, in the navy, those creaky albatross
I'd tossed Tabasco-sauced bread to
from the fantail of our ship. Mindless

and cruel, beauty was the last thing
I think I would have ever thought of.

So why was I thinking of it now
and staying up all night to find it?
Whatever it was that made the hair

on the back of my arms stand up
and that darkness in the window

in the merest blinking of an eye
to somehow disappear—leaving me
at a card table in an old coal bin

with one bare bulb hanging down . . .
I can remember thinking, even then

how it could have been a jail cell
a room where prisoners were tortured
the last place on God's grim earth

where poetry might happen. And yet
now and then, rising up from nowhere

on slowly beating wings, something—
I knew there was something, born
perhaps of the heart's pure yearning

that would save my life: Beauty.
The name for those birds was Beauty.

TOOLS AND PROVISIONS

One lucky summer in college
I found a job building shelves
in a deep-freeze warehouse.

Every morning, I remember
I had to dress like Shackleton—
snow boots, navy surplus parka . . .

And it was hard, with gloves on
to grip those power tools right—
the drill and slippery wrench

the treacherous, screw–loose saw
that kept on getting stuck—
so I mostly worked bare–handed

until my hands would freeze . . .
Then I'd have to go on break
back into the staggering, camel–

killing heat of the loading dock
too stiff–fingered to unzip myself
or even light a cigarette, Camels—

it troubles me now to remember—
the kind I smoked back then
in that heroic, adventurous life.

I can see myself as clearly there
as in a photograph: the dock
busy with men and provisions

broken pallets, dollies, and boxes . . .
And there I am, in the foreground—
a young man zipped up in a parka

looking both frozen and sun–struck
a cigarette dangling from his lip
his eyes small slits in that light

as if he were trying somehow
to make out what it was exactly
that seemed to be approaching there—

those little dots on the horizon . . .
An island perhaps. The rescue ship.
A raft of ice with walrus on it . . .

Or perhaps a caravan of some kind—
Bedouin camel traders, rug merchants
pilgrims on their way to Mecca . . .

Until the boss himself shows up.
He wants a place by noon to stack
a whole truckload of french fries.

After that, a shelf for onion rings.
And just for the record, he's not
paying me, college boy that I am

to sit around on my ass all day
and daydream. And that was it—
back to my tools and two–by–fours

the frozen gloom of the warehouse
littered with sawdust, like snow
and loose, occasional french fries

that could startle me sometimes
as if I'd found a human finger there . . .
One of mine, of course, sawn off

in some momentary fit of drowsiness.
It was certainly possible. It was
simply a question of time I thought

drilling four quick holes for the bolts
and bolting that fact to the wall—
planking the hull of my provisional ark.

THE SAILBOAT MOVIE

The sailboat was brand new
so they were being careful—

a heavy, middle–aged man
and his nervous, younger wife.

You could tell they'd never
backed it into the water before.

He was having a hard time
keeping the trailer straight

while she rode in the boat
and shouted out directions:

Hold it! It's crooked again!
More to the left next time!

so that next time of course
backing hard to port, one wheel

bangs off the side of the ramp
and almost knocks her to her knees—

her look in that quick instant
reminding me of some old movie

I can't remember quite, although
a typhoon comes vividly to mind—

a sailboat pounded by huge waves
you could only see by lightning

that cracking loudly lit as well
the heroine, grasping at the rail

her mouth agape in sudden horror
as her alcoholic, captain husband

steers them on the rocks somewhere
in the dead middle of the ocean.

But I forget what happens next . . .
Except, had this been real life

they would have drowned for sure—
drowned, become food for the fish

or otherwise atomically dispersed
throughout the void and deep abyss

of the real–life ocean. Not exactly
what we go to movies for. Instead

I think they probably washed ashore
on some lovely, south–sea island

where, after awhile, they manage
to fix the boat and sail off again

with an incidental fortune in pearls
for England or maybe San Francisco . . .

Someplace more romantic certainly
than here, on the launching ramp

of windless, swampy hot Lake Mingo
in real–life, east–central Illinois

where now, after an hour or so
of collapsing bumper jacks, levers

and sweaty, pissed–off struggle
a brand–new sister sloop of sorts

is finally floating in the oily
still, Lake Mingo Marina lagoon.

It's going to take a little while
before they learn to sail this thing—

port, starboard, fore and aft . . .
all that vocabulary to memorize

not to mention the various knots
and rigging procedures. Meanwhile

he's trying to get them untied
from the mooring cleat, his shorts

as he bends over exposing three
or four inches of sudden cleavage

at which she startles, speechless—
as if a giant tentacle of some kind

(the octopus that guards the pearls!)
had wrapped itself around the mast

with a mind to pull them under . . .
But when I look again, she's started

up their little outboard motor . . .
And a happy puttering, like music

signaling THE END in movies maybe
rises to its passionate crescendo—

whisking them off into the future
on a cloud of bluish smoke, a future

where the sky is incidentally green
right now, green and getting darker.

SLEEP STUDY

It seems he snores
like a water buffalo

and sometimes in his sleep
for long, anxious intervals
before he's poked awake again

stops breathing altogether . . .
as if indeed he might be dead—

or, as another theory has it
traveling as an astral spirit
on furlough from mortality . . .

And so, for the sake of science
he allows himself to be hooked up

to a kind of ectoplasmic fax machine
for a procedure the doctor calls
"a sleep study." His least breath

his every twitch, strictly monitored
the whole night long, his dreams

graphed and measured for intensity—
the sloshing of his very bowels
revealing secrets for all he knows

as darkly telling as the guts
of strangled doves in ancient Rome.

But because he's left a window open
that was now impossible to close—
encumbered as he was by an octopus

of feedback cable—he finds himself
between one breath and the next

on a hillside in Bosnia somewhere
half-frozen and watching a donkey
trapped in a snarl of barbed wire.

Every time it staggers, kicks
its one free foot, a land mine

explodes in the rocks nearby . . .
He likes the sound of it, the wispy
quick drift of smoke reminding him

of fireworks at first . . . as if
in fact, there's still some chance

he might be dreaming: mittens, shoes
those pale bodies tangled in the weeds . . .
but then, like a stifled exhalation

a nasal rattling of little stones
and fecal mud come raining down

as if to prove he's really there
and witness in his footloose apnea
to stupid war, plague, and famine—

the same apocalypse as advertised
each evening on the late–night news . . .

followed by the weather, sports
and a National Geographic maybe
featuring sharks, Kodiak bears

or, under the heaped Antarctic ice
at the howling foot of Mount Eberus

the ghostly emperor penguin again
flying like an ordinary bird almost
over his dead–still anemone garden—

another brave soul like himself
exploring the underworld of sleep . . .

each wing beat stirring up a blizzard
of images, a kind of plankton cloud
of old photographs, lost pictures

of his dead father, for instance—
his brother, even that snapshot

of a child looking up from underwater
in last night's paper, his eyes
wide open, his too familiar face

comically distended like someone
playing a joke perhaps, just holding

his breath awhile in some monsoon
and tide-filled ditch in Bangladesh
beside his bloated water buffalo.

FRIGHT TRAIN

> They merely observed the night sky until
> the constellation of the Pleiades passed the
> zenith. Then "they knew . . ." Nonetheless,
> the world was thought to be still in jeopardy,
> and it was then that they acted, one priest
> making a fire on the breast of an illustrious
> captive.
> —Inga Clenndinnen, *Aztecs*

Tonight, the late-night news begins
with footage of a huge, black funnel
descending on a row of mobile homes

and then, dreamlike, they all explode
or seem to, into clouds of loose debris—

until the camera too goes flying
and we're lost awhile in darkness
as if behind the closed-shut eyes

of someone who survives this thing
or doesn't, depending on the next

few bricks from the undone barbecue
or a motorboat perhaps, sailing in
through the front room window . . .

It sounded, I hear a woman saying
as the light comes flickering back

just like a big ol' fright train
her country accent flat with shock
her eyes still focused on the Void

which looked, when lightning flashed
like an ordinary kitchen I suppose

but situated inside a railroad tunnel
or someplace even more unfortunate—
like that bakery, say, in Sarajevo

where everyone gets blown to pieces
right after the next commercial . . .

But meanwhile, the camera dithers
and dilates here, amid the rubble
of the Aztec Valley Trailer Court

noticing, as if possibly significant
the curious abundance of underwear

or now, under the wrecked motorboat
an almost tragic, but thank Christ
finally sentimental, bent tricycle.

The fact that no one died of course
is simply unaccountable, a miracle

or fluke of quantum physics maybe
whereby straws are sometimes driven
into trees, teacups left undisturbed

while the house around them disappears
into nothing at all. Thus, the massive

architecture of archaic Tenochtitlan
and the gods who fed on human hearts—
like Huizilopchtli, fast–twittering

"Hummingbird on the Left" whose wings
at the close of the Old Bundle of Years

must have fluttered terribly indeed
above the shrieking of his victims—
a sound like a mortar round perhaps

exploding forever in a brick schoolyard
or a fright train on the evening news.

GARAGE

There are no doors on this garage
and the roof is full of holes
through which the winter sunlight

as the planet tilts toward dusk
falls briefly incandescent for awhile
on something red or cobalt blue

or dazzles on a piece of chrome,
green bottle shards, parts of things
forever nameless at this distance . . .

which isn't far at all—a short jog
just off the road in fact. Still
why should someone take the trouble

and then be disappointed? Cat piss
certainly. Old shingles. A broken
bag of gray cement . . . or even worse

a wad of dirty blankets, empty cans—
evidence that someone sleeps there
now and then, a few bright stars

like tinfoil crib or playpen toys
burning briefly incandescent overhead.
And where's the house? From the way

the brush and trees have taken over
it must have burned down years ago.
Burned down, collapsed, blown away . . .

although it was probably never much
to start with. Look at this garage
for instance, the few poor things

that burn forever nameless there
like baubles on a Christmas tree—
whatever anyone could make by hand

out of nothing, because the children
after all, liked that sort of thing—
all those brilliant colors the brain

like some dark garage, keeps secret
until the morphine alone can kill you
or a heart monitor goes suddenly flat

one afternoon in Florida let's say
where it's probably raining, gray—
the bedside flowers indistinguishable.

4

GHOST

Coming in from the morning's run
sweaty but not tired, feeling better
really, than I have for years

adolescent, even, in my specific
and innocent thirst for orange juice
after three whole weeks of not drinking

I catch, just barely audible at first
over the cold hum of the refrigerator
an arrhythmic, suspicious fluttering

from down in the basement somewhere—
a frayed belt on the washing machine
a part working loose in the dryer . . .

followed by the unmistakable thump
of something soft hitting a window—
something alive and fluttering again

in the ductwork above the furnace . . .
a bird of course. A starling finally
dragging a huge, claw–footed shadow

from window to window, wrestling it
from pipe to flue, croaking a little
in his terror, like one of the damned

who, having fallen in this instance
down the black hole of our chimney
finds himself floundering in the gloom

of another whole universe entirely—
an underworld of gray cement in fact
redolent of mildew, old laundry, dreams

in which I keep hearing tiny noises
and then find my dead brother again
hiding in the furnace with a shotgun.

Just now, however, in this wide–awake
absolutely sober, forty–watt flashback
of the actual suicide basement, he seems

to be a bird. As a child, I remember
he was always jumping off of things—
couches, porch rails, the garage roof . . .

so perhaps it's perfectly natural now
for him to be a bird, confused like this
with no memory at all of the old life—

neither the porch, nor the rose of Sharon
he sailed right over in his wash–towel cape.
Not his mother, not his father passed out

snoring on the swing. And not me certainly
watching my brother as he asked me to—
drinking my juice at the top of our steps.

PERISCOPE

Waiting for sleep
and aimlessly adrift
on the wine–lulled sea

of late middle age—
my own dark ship

rising and falling
in undulant doldrum
on the bibulous deep—

I find that often now
I've drifted back to 1958

and the South China Sea
where I'm nineteen again . . .
a yawning midwatch lookout

on the *USS Regulus,* AF 57—
a tublike refrigeration ship

Joseph Conrad would have loved
right down to the dull romance
of being repeatedly torpedoed

by any friendly submarine
that needed target practice.

But for my part, I preferred
just sort of looking around
through my feckless binoculars

at all the unguessable stars
of the Malay Archipelago.

Recklessly adrift one minute
with everything there was
to do or dream or be, then

lost again as merest plankton
amid the dangerous menagerie

of the southern constellations,
it's no wonder on occasion
a sudden phosphorescent torpedo

off our port or starboard bow
escaped my notice entirely . . .

but for those keeping score
of course, sending our ship
theoretically to the bottom.

Holy jumping Christ! Send that
asshole up here on the double!

And yet, after all these years
those same stars and meteors
even the squat *Regulus* herself

rolling along at fourteen knots
in fat silhouette on the horizon

still appear to me sometimes
before sleep, in perfect focus—
but slightly magnified too

and just a little tilted maybe
as if I were in a wave trough

or otherwise below the horizon
and looking out from that angle
through my binoculars again—

or, more oddly still
through a periscope somehow . . .

There she is: her cargo masts
and hopeless three-inch guns—
her lookout talking to himself

singing . . . Is he allowed to smoke?
How young he looks! How innocent!

And how swiftly as the years
are those torpedoes streaking
toward him, fore and aft.

SURVIVORS

We're sitting in his living room
having coffee
        surrounded by cats:

myself
        self–importantly in town
for a conference
        and my old best friend
from college—
        half poet
        half criminal—
who I haven't seen in thirty years . . .

"Cats are great survivors," he says—
carefully
        arthritically lifting meanwhile
a gray
        ear–torn tomcat to his lap . . .

"This tough guy here for instance
grew up in the woods."

        Which is how
I think
        given his own generic history
of bad marriages
        alcohol and drugs—

that long litany of compulsive fault
familiar
        and horrific all at once—

he'd like to think of himself:
                a man
completely independent
             self–reliant—
the tough guy who lands on his feet . . .

And then of course
          while his third
or fourth wife putters in the kitchen
pretending not to listen
            it's my turn—

as if this ritual impulse
          to confess
three whole decades of stray regret
and nine–lived
        alley–cat insouciance

conferred
        beyond a sense of feral kinship
in the mazy woods
        of mere survival
a kind of winking absolution . . .

After which
           we're back outside again
promising to write
               shaking hands
in the driveway—
                completely

at a loss for things to say—
                       until finally
after a long time
              of embarrassed
speechless looking down
                    he stoops
and picks up something
                     interesting
from the grass:
            an egg . . .

a windfall robin's egg—
                    that happiest
of all things blue—
                amazingly intact
even after last night's storm
among the knocked–down daffodils . . .

"A little something," he says
                    winking
and handing it over
                  "to remember me by"—
a metaphor
          for sheer dumb luck perhaps . . .

a metaphor
        whose faint florescence
on the long trip home
          trembles
in an ashtray
       beneath the lurid
industrial nimbus
        of nighttime Gary
Chicago
     and orange–lit Kankakee . . .

where I have to stop awhile
         half–blind
from headlight glare
        in some anonymous
truck–loud rest area . . .

and end up sleeping finally—
         or rather
fitfully pursuing it
       from one bad dream
to another—

       each waking interval
punctuated by the *thud*
       thud thud
of someone's rude
      incessant radio . . .

and other sounds besides:
                              voices
odd scraps of conversation
                              that seemed
uncanny echoes
                    of just–fled dreams somehow . . .

until
          the egg itself starts speaking—
or peeping anyway—
                              a sound I thought
for sure
               was coming from the ashtray
something
               in code I thought

some message
                    I had to strain hard
to hear
               above the *thud*
                              thud thud
of my own quick heartbeat . . .

while everywhere
                    through windows
                                        and doors
even up through the floor
                              the gray light
of a perfectly
                    ordinary consciousness
like icy water
                    comes rushing in . . .

And then I'm listening
                    to a bird somewhere
other voices
              the sound
                      of someone's radio . . .

a bird's egg meanwhile
                    like the small
blue echo
          of some perfect innocence
I can't remember,
                another planet

that looks exactly like this one—
but as God himself might see it
from far
          far out in outer space—

resting still unbroken
                    in my ashtray.

A GAY AND DISTANT MUSIC

> That time is past,
> And all its aching joys are now no more,
> And all its dizzy raptures.
> —Wordsworth, "Tintern Abbey"

It's just the end of August
but up here, at the very tip
of Michigan's upper peninsula

it's fall already, cold rain
blowing in from Lake Superior.

I've driven up here on a whim
from Illinois, to see the town
where my mother was born . . .

twenty or twenty–five houses
four blocks from end to end

and then the lake, green–gray
foaming in the rocks down there
a hundred feet or so below me.

Where is everyone? Nothing doing
but some seagulls now, and a dog

monotonous, barking far away . . .
a metronome almost, keeping time
for that lugubrious door perhaps

creaking in the ruined smelter
just behind me—a note teetering

just now, after two days in the car
with a radio or tape deck playing,
on the sheer brink of absence itself . . .

Not at all the way my mother still
remembers it. Every Fourth of July

the town would hold its picnic here.
Her father, a cook for lumber camps
would cook for the whole town . . .

You can't imagine the excitement.
There was a Ferris wheel, fireworks—

then dancing on a wooden platform.
Someone Polish played the accordion . . .
Oh, you know, my mother might say

confusing me with God knows who—
old what's–his–name, you know

the one who got crushed to death
down in that mine at Calumet . . .
Then she'd talk about the snow

and the winter she didn't starve
because her mother owned a cow.

Diphtheria, typhoid, lice . . .
It seemed a miracle anyone survived
beyond the age of twelve up here.

And yet, this persistent, gay
nostalgia. Or, as Wordsworth

might have put it, that curious
"sense sublime / Of something
far more deeply interfused . . ."

Meanwhile, the wind's picked up
and slams that iron door again—

again, like some impatient child
who thinks we should be leaving
for Detroit by now, someplace fun

where maybe she could find a job
or even go to school. The house

where the dog lives, by the way
has a highway sign in the window:
LEAVING GAY, it says. After that

a long stretch of empty highway
without any irony whatsoever.

VERMEER

For awhile
            after my father died
my clearest
            most dreamlike memory

recalled him in his yellow bathrobe
and sitting at the kitchen table
playing solitaire—
            inscrutable
sunlight glinting off his glasses
as in a painting maybe
            by Vermeer . . .

one indecisive hand
            floating
like some incongruous
            white bird
over the angled rows of cards—

red on black
            black on red
following the floor and countertops
back into the diminishing perspectives
of some forgotten
            winter afternoon
from my childhood in Detroit . . .

But outside
                and without contradiction
the way things happen in our dreams
I know it's Florida
                    the last summer
of his retirement before he dies . . .

In the backyard
                    heavy with fruit
the lime
            orange
                    and grapefruit trees
are bending to the ground . . .

the veritable trees of Paradise
of course
                but left unpainted
by Vermeer
                who preferred the temporal
the indoors
                and small enigmas
like my father playing solitaire . . .

a man you wouldn't dare disturb
with idle conversation—
                            laid–off
on strike
            or even fired this time
considering the way his jaw is set . . .

though there's something wistful too
distant

        pensive in the way his head
is tilted slightly

           as if outside

on snowy Gratiot Avenue

               he might
be listening to another streetcar
pass sadly out of hearing

               with a sigh . . .

Or perhaps the trees of Paradise
were whispering in the wind—
the white bird

        of his daydreams
hovering above them

              like a ghostly
hand almost

        unable to choose
among so much fruit . . .

But whatever it is

         when I look back
I see he's utterly absorbed again—
like the very dust

        floating
in that lambent air—

            by light itself.

BREAKING UP THE BODY

Somewhere in the labyrinth
of yards across the alley
a dog has whined and barked

all day in the stuporous heat
and now a family of sparrows

seems to be having an argument
under the air conditioner
in my study window . . . that

or they're being attacked
by something—some vague

Platonic silhouette perhaps
encoded in their DNA, a stick
they've never seen before

that's managed nonetheless
to climb the rainspout . . .

What a racket! Those shrill
falsetto peeps, those frail
wings beating against metal . . .

They sound like someone's old
old mom in fact, yelling

on the telephone: *Absolutely
not! Never! I'd rather die
than live in that dumb home!*

Besides which, the ne'er–do–well
who brought it up sounds drunk

and just exactly like his father
except he's ten times meaner
and only cares about her money.

After that of course we both
hang up. The air conditioner

kicks back in again and things
more or less go on as usual.
Downstairs, when I go down

Some crocodiles are eating
a wildebeest on television.

It's fascinating. From time
to time one or another of them
lifts its head from the water

and swallows huge chunks of it—
a foreleg, a whole hindquarter . . .

"Breaking up the body," it's called—
a thrashing, twisting maneuver
peculiar to their species . . .

And then I'm disturbed to notice
it's almost dark outside—time

for the animals to gather, time
for my anxious thoughts to gather
at some remembered waterhole . . .

as in that labyrinth of cicada
throbbing trees across the alley

my mother feeds the dog again
calls the children in to supper
or runs cold water in a tub

as if it were perfectly natural
since the time we lived in trees

to do these things—the trees
all humming meanwhile, incessant
as the background radiation

of the void.

IN THE COMPANY OF MANATEES

> The samurai looks insignificant
> beside his armor of black dragon scales.
> —Tomas Tranströmer, "After a Death"

One by one, every ten minutes
or so by my watch, the manatees
at the Tampa Zoo float slowly up

like tiny, one-man subs for air . . .
and then, their dive tanks flooding
to a delicate, negative buoyancy

sink, at one half-foot per second
to just within their body's width
of bottom—no longer submarines

at all, but stumps of driftwood
seawrack now, without one hint
of sentience or least volition . . .

unless, of course, one counts
at the foggy observation window
all their several amputations

and propeller scars—evidence
that might just point to something
darkly headlong in their nature

or warlike and ferocious even . . .
until they look like samurai almost—
but dazed, adrift in shock somehow

lost in the dreamy aftermath perhaps
of some great slaughter. What mercies
might their enemies expect after all

face to face with these grim veterans—
so calm, so *still* in their nicked–up
crisscrossed, black dragon armor!

Otherwise, that thumping roar outside
is probably not an air raid, artillery
or ski boats blowing up in Tampa harbor

but rather, an ordinary bulldozer
clearing ground for a new addition—
another wing for the gravely wounded

like the one who floats above me now
eating lettuce in a corner, her tail
lopped and short a starboard flipper.

A civilian obviously. An orphaned
adolescent, no larger than my daughter
who keeps on looking at her watch, bored

and grounded here with her dim parents
all afternoon between planes, a hurricane
still threatening in the aviary palms . . .

She'd rather be skiing, of course—
at dusk, among the dangerous mangroves.
She's thinking, I know, of the smooth

black water, the way it feels, her skis
chattering over it for miles and miles . . .
She can't stand this sitting still.

Nor has she ever seen those clouds
of sudden blood that sometimes blossom
close behind us in this headlong life.

Her own sweet limbs and spirit still
intact, her own bad dreams just dreams,
how can I explain what keeps me here

among these submarines and samurai
these poor, maimed beasts come back
. . . from where? In all their terrible

unforgiving innocence.

TWILIGHT OF THE NEANDERTHALS

for Louis Jenkins

I. FOG

The rain has finally stopped
and now a cold fog has settled
over the burned-out forest
where we have come to gather

firewood, I think . . . or maybe
berries of some kind.
                              Up ahead
I can hear the dangerous water
rushing loudly over stones . . .

and beyond that, crows again
arguing our intentions here—
which are not clear,
                              not clear . . .

being one more instance merely
of an inveterate forgetfulness
for which we have no adequate
language,
                    only the monosyllabic
smell of ashes and scorched trees—

the acrid, pungent grammar
of the afternoon itself,
                              the dead
dendritic thickets of some lost
connection here . . .
                              wherein
bereft alike of sunlight, syntax
or even brute analogy, we stumble

from one amnesia to another . . .

unable to distinguish finally
between mastodons made entirely
of fog
      and the real catastrophe.

2. ARITHMETIC

How is it
      that we never learned
to count?
      How is it, nonetheless
that some of us seem always
to be missing?
      I remember
watching a mother duck once
swimming in a weedy estuary
with her babies . . . then
      half asleep
being startled by a loud splash—
sploosh! as if someone had thrown
a rock in the water—
      followed
by a quacking, two–second flurry
of duck–motherly consternation . . .

which meant that one of them
was missing of course,
      or even
more . . . But on the other hand
without being able to count
how could she ever be sure?

And so she sensibly
                    forgets it
and preens herself instead—
reassured, calmed in an instant
by the lively,
                    hysterical peeping
of those who were spared . . .

curiously unlike ourselves
for whom the dead are never
simply absent,
                    but experienced
rather more the way old hunters
feel pain for years sometimes
in a chewed–off arm or leg.

Or suppose this very afternoon
near the riverbank
                    in the fog
we heard the sound of something
heavy falling into water . . .
                              then
screams,
          indicating one of us—
who also never learned to swim.

Ridiculous to think it doesn't
make a difference
                    beyond all number.

And besides,
          we have the body
which must be buried with masses
of flowers, masses of flowers . . .

or left for the animals.

3. CRO-MAGNONS

Friends they say,
                   cousins even
who come to us from the south
with tools and valuable skills . . .

When game is scarce,
                   they know
how to set the forest on fire
and where to wait in ambush

for whatever squealing thing
half-cooked
                and barely alive
they can kill with a stick . . .

And sometimes they have dreams
that tell them
                where the swift
uncatchable horses are grazing—
aurochs and great woolly mammoths

they drive by the herd
                   over cliffs
killing them all—
                until finally
they've even terrified themselves

and thus must ask forgiveness
of the dead—
                recreating them
by torch light
                in bright ocher
on the walls of our mutual cave . . .

or, as happens more
                    and more
frequently of late,
                    in rooms
far, far back in the labyrinth
where we are not allowed—

rooms echoing with high–pitched
little bone whistles,
                    drums
screams they refuse to explain . . .

although afterwards
                    some of us
seem always to be missing.

Caught in the open
                    they'll say
by a bungled grass fire.
                              Lost
on the glacier,
                    buried forever
in the avalanche . . .
                    accidents
that only they have witnessed.

And no doubt because our grief
annoys them
                    we are sometimes
given strange, medicinal herbs
to help us forget—
                    potions
engendering uncomfortable dreams—

dreams of walking through fog,
dreams of the burned–out forest . . .

and lately,

            recurring dreams
of food . . .

         or rather,

                  bones merely—

belonging to some delicious animal
we can't remember eating,

                        of course.

SHANGRI-LA

By ten o'clock the snow
has stopped and a west wind
has pushed the clouds apart

exposing little bits of sky
like ponds of windswept ice

where now and then Orion
or some other constellation
drifts partly into view . . .

No traffic. No sounds at all
except the dog, snuffling along

delirious, through the powdery
chest–deep snow of Shangri–la
for all she knows . . . And then

quick as a rabbit, the moon
breaks free again, followed

closely by a star—the merest
tooth or lynx–bright eye perhaps
of something still ineffable—

cruel as the gravity in dreams
of running nowhere in deep snow . . .

But for one skipped heartbeat
with clouds in sudden wisps
like underwater blood almost

swirling darkly out behind them
how fast they both seem moving!

An illusion so convincing, even
the dog takes notice—barking
furiously, every hair electric

the way she barks each morning
at mostly phantom garbage men

or birds, the very light itself—
some world she still remembers
from fifty million years ago . . .

A feeling I'll share tomorrow
reading the paper at breakfast

in the busy student union—
the talk around me adolescent
suburban in its accent

and focused mainly on the weather
like all the front–page pictures

in the paper: stranded motorists
buried cars . . . then, on page two
a photograph that seems at first

to be a shot of absolutely nothing—
a blank hillside of trampled snow

that turns out to be a creek bank
in that very park we walked through—
a weedless slope some homeless drunk

had tumbled down, over and over
again, invisibly drowning finally

without a name, at the bottom
of the page—my dog still barking
for all I know. How strange

listening to the talk around me
so feckless, so immortal really

to think he might have heard her
and seen the naked moon like that
swiftly, swiftly going nowhere.

THE LAST NEANDERTHAL

Browsing in the waiting room
through dog–eared *Time,* he reads
how all over the world, frogs

are disappearing—a thinning
it's supposed, of the ozone . . .

and then it's his turn. Blood
pressure, prostate palpation . . .
followed by the usual questions:

Any . . . um . . . trouble getting it up?
Painful or bloody urination?

Not so far. But one day, he thinks
it could all be different. The light
becoming suddenly brighter, ominous

and the doctor frowning meanwhile
snapping off his rubber gloves . . .

After that, surgery, chemotherapy
the rest of his life in diapers . . .
But for now, except for a niggling

slight elevation in blood pressure
he's OK and deserves a handshake:

Keep up the good work. Exercise.
And take this form to the front desk.
We need your group insurance number.

And soon he's driving home again
curiously aware of the littered

roadside, the look of late March—
blossoms of Styrofoam and paper cups
shivering in the stiff, brown bushes

while overhead drift clouds of lead—
a sky that might rain anything:

dead dogs and cats for instance—
car junk, disemboweled sofas . . . even
the radio stinks. Continual static

interrupting a talk show of some kind.
Some paleoanthropologist it seems

talking about our human origins—
and people calling in with questions:
What about those Neanderthals then?

*Were they human or not? And why
if they were as smart as you seem*

*to think, did they all die out?
OK. I'll hang up now and listen.*
At which point, the station disappears

and there's nothing on the air again
but noise, a sound like leaves perhaps

rattling in an empty cave somewhere
along the Rhine . . . It's almost dark.
Nearby, the last Neanderthal hunkers

over a small fire, roasting a frog
on a stick. A man much like himself

but bigger and covered with hair—
his low forehead wrinkled suddenly
by something he hears out there . . .

a car whizzing by in another dimension.
It's possible. If he can imagine it

why not? Meanwhile, the frog
looks almost done. A small frog
the size of a baseball or an enlarged

prostate maybe. He can see it clearly.
A middle–aged man much like himself.

ACKNOWLEDGMENTS

Grateful acknowledgment is made to the following publications in which some of the poems in this collection first appeared: *American Literary Review* ("Guardian Angel"); *Arkansas Review* ("Sleep Study," "Survivors"); *Cimarron Review* ("Beauty," "Garage," "Tools and Provisions"); *Controlled Burn* ("Clarity"); *Crazy Horse* ("Cuckoo," "Fright Train"); *Gettysburg Review* ("Perpetual Motion," "The Sailboat Movie"); *Southern Review* ("Shangri–La," "Twilight of the Neanderthals," "Vermeer"); *Sou'wester* ("In the Company of Manatees"); *Willow Springs* ("The Elephant in Winter," "Periscope," "Startled Awake Once More in the City of Dreams," "Two Seizures").

"Ghost" and "The Last Neanderthal" first appeared in the *Hudson Review.*

The author also thanks the Illinois Arts Council for their generous support during the writing of this book.

Michael Van Walleghen received his B.A. in English
from Wayne State University in Detroit and his M.F.A.
in Creative Writing from the University of Iowa. He is
the author of four previous books of poetry: *The
Wichita Poems* (1975); *More Trouble with the Obvious* (1981),
winner of the 1980 Lamont Poetry Prize of the Acad-
emy of American Poets; *Blue Tango* (1989); and *Tall Birds
Stalking* (1994). Van Walleghen is a professor of English
at the University of Illinois, Urbana-Champaign, where
he lives with his wife and daughter.

Library of Congress Cataloging-in-Publication Data
Van Walleghen, Michael, 1938–
    The last Neanderthal / Michael Van Walleghen.
          p.   cm. —   (Pitt poetry series)
    ISBN 0-8229-5696-9 (pbk. : acid-free paper)
    I. Title. II. Series.
PS3572.A545 L37 1999
811'.54—dc21   98-40137